Intentional

ISBN: 979-8-9870337-1-5

52 Maxims of Conscious Choosing

To Create the Deeply Satisfying
Life You Desire

Becky Henderson, MA, LPC

This book belongs to:

_____

The adventure begins:

_____

Everything can be taken from a man
but one thing:
the last of the human freedoms —
to choose one's attitude
in any given set of circumstances,
to choose one's own way.

— Viktor E. Frankl

Man's Search for Meaning

Intentional
STARTS HERE

Welcome, fellow adventurer.

The deeply satisfying life you desire does not happen by default.

It is created.

It is renewed daily, continually.

It

is

Intentional.

Human beings are choice-making creatures. We are never not choosing. Perhaps you have heard the axiom that even not choosing is a choice. We make thousands of choices a day. Most of these choices are unconscious, having formed into automatic habits through training and repetition. For many situations, unconscious choosing is actually efficient; it helps with productivity, performance, and mastery of skills. But by the time we reach adulthood, we're so good at unconscious choosing that life often turns into a rinse-and-repeat existence, where today looks pretty much as yesterday did, which looked like the day before *that*, which looked like the day before *that*...

week after week.............

month after month.............

year after year.............

There are unconscious, outdated choices running your life right now. Unconscious choosing can and will deliver only one thing...more of the life you already have. It has no capacity to help you generate anything new. So when the life you desire is other than the life you are living, it is time to get conscious with your choosing. For it is in *conscious* choosing that your capacity to generate something new is engaged. Conscious choosing is the path to create deep satisfaction in your life and it requires that you be intentional.

Don't confuse being intentional with having good intentions. Good intentions are pretty impotent in and of themselves; they are thoughts and ideas that often don't accomplish desired outcomes. To be intentional is to move beyond ideas into deliberate, committed actions that produce the results you desire.

Intentional presents you with fifty-two choices regarding your relationships with yourself, with others, and with the resources (time, money, health, etc.) that sustain you. These fifty-two choices are not random, nor are they designed to give you merely a *different* life; they are purposed to give you access to a *new and deeply satisfying* life by actualizing what matters to you. This new life is created through new choices that only you can make for yourself.

Now, it is very common to wait for circumstances to (magically) change in order to make new choices. This kind of waiting often amounts to perpetual delay and frustration—it's exhausting. However, as a human being, you have the capacity and power to move through the world in a much more dynamic, exhilarating, and thrilling way.

Rather than delaying new choices until you get new circumstances, you can get new circumstances by making new choices. In other words, new choices will make the changes you are waiting for. You can stop waiting and start choosing...intentionally. I hope that sounds like good news!

It may be tempting on a journey of conscious choosing to judge your current reality as bad or wrong in order to justify making a choice for something new. Keep in mind that the choices you make throughout your life are largely informed by the season you are in at the time you make them.

New choices will make the changes you are waiting for.

By season, I don't mean stages of human development or yearly weather patterns. The season I'm referring to is whatever happens to be important to you—whatever you value—during a particular period of time. Here's an example: You could live many years in a season of "I must be liked and accepted by others" and make choices according to what you think will win others' approval. Then one day you could suddenly shift into a season of "I really am okay whether others accept me or not," where you start making decisions free from the concern of others' approval.

This is how seasons often work in human life:
the old gives way to the emergence of the new.

Sometimes the shift is sudden and abrupt, and sometimes the shift is gradual and progressive. Since you are dealing with seasons, there is no need to judge your current life as bad or wrong in order to choose something new. That kind of judgment is completely unnecessary and likely to interfere with new growth.

To be alive is to grow, emerge,
release, and transform.

The pull you are experiencing for newness in your life is not evidence that the current season is bad; it is life's signal that the current season is ending and the next season is beginning. Consider that the dissatisfaction you have with your current circumstances is life's way of readying you to grow beyond who you are right now.

Life has something new for you.
Life in you wants to grow, emerge,
release, and transform.
So take a breath.
Relax.

Trust that life is signaling your next new season.

The Innovator
LEADER

Intentional was written for a particular kind of person: The Innovator Leader. You may be wondering, "Who is that?" or "Am I The Innovator Leader?" or even "Will this book help me if I'm not?" Perhaps you've never considered yourself an innovator or a leader before. It might surprise you, after reading the description, to discover that The Innovator Leader could, in fact, be you. And yes, *Intentional* is designed to be incredibly useful to you, even if you don't identify as The Innovator Leader. More on that will follow.

So, who is The Innovator Leader?

Not all innovators are leaders, and not all leaders are innovators. As The Innovator Leader, you are uniquely both. You perceive life through two sets of lenses simultaneously: fully Innovator, fully Leader, all the time.

You see possibilities the rest of the world just doesn't see... yet, and you care so much for others that you make it your mission to help them get there. You are fueled by a deep sense of purpose at home, at work, and in your community. You can be found in any role and position—employee, boss, spouse, parent, student, mentor, friend, citizen, etc. With and without titles, you listen, you serve, and you cultivate greatness in humanity.

Your biggest frustration is that you often find yourself burdened with too many demands and not enough of what it takes to fulfill them. Rather than spend your energy battling the scarcity, strain, and stagnation that constantly get in your way, your soul craves to deliver your greatest service and fulfill your biggest visions from a place of true well-being and plenty. This is the deeply satisfying life you desire.

Does that sound like you? I wrote *Intentional* specifically to help you break free from the constraints holding you back so that you can share more of what you're truly capable of with the world. Imagine the world we would have with more Innovator Leaders like you who are liberated to thrive while passionately pursuing their mission.

Now, what if you've made it this far and *don't* see yourself as The Innovator Leader? Good news! *Intentional* will help anyone committed to creating a deeply satisfying life, and that pursuit is not exclusive to The Innovator Leader. As human beings, regardless of our positions and purposes, we possess an innate drive to surpass our current limitations and create an abundance of what truly matters to us. Unfortunately, far too many have grown frustrated and given up on making that a reality. But not you! You are actively seeking to create that reality, and *Intentional* will serve you powerfully on your journey. Imagine the world we would have with more people like you who are thrilled to be alive and intentionally creating a life they love.

USING

Intentional

- Mental health disclaimer: *Intentional* is purposed for personal and professional *self*-development only, not professional therapy, counseling, or professional coaching. Should you choose to use *Intentional* as an adjunct to therapy or coaching, do so in cooperation with your therapist or coach. You get to take full responsibility for your own well-being and use of this material.

- *Intentional* is designed for you to focus on and practice one new choice a week for one year. Each choice includes a passage of principles and a set of questions to help you integrate the choice into your daily experience.

- *Intentional* is not meant to be read; it is meant to be lived. It is not meant for accumulating more conceptual knowledge; it is designed for creating living experiences. The power to bring forth something new in your life through this material lies in your *direct experience* with each new choice, not in the *idea* of the new choice alone.

Aren't you tired of going through book after book
or course after course
and not seeing one bit of difference in your life?

Don't. Do. That. Here.

You must get with each choice—move, wrestle, dance, and play with it—in order to get anything worthwhile from the knowledge contained herein.

Experiment.

Discover.

Practice.

Grow.

Give yourself the time and space to go beyond merely reading and thinking about the new choice. Make an appointment on your calendar to practice each choice and keep it. Action is where miracles happen. Be in action like your life depends on it because the life you desire actually does.

- I *highly* recommend you use a journal to process and record your experience with each choice. Spend at least five minutes a day writing out—in words, pictures, or both—your experience of putting each choice into practice in your life. What ideas, inspirations, fears, and objections come up in you?

What worked?

What didn't work?

What did you notice?

What did you learn?

- Approach each choice as if you have never considered it before. Set aside the opinions, thoughts, conclusions, and judgments you may have previously formed about it—what you like or don't like, what's possible or not possible, what works or doesn't work.

  Bring a sense of wonder to discover new dimensions about any choice you deem as having already figured out. Come newly, with fresh curiosity, to explore what each choice could mean for you *right now*.

- The visual layout of *Intentional* is...intentional. It is designed to increase your conscious attention by slowing down the rate at which you consume this work. It operates like a speed bump. There are things for you to notice and think deeply about that are only available to you at a slower pace. You may experience it as irritation, but it will cause your brain to process the information differently from how it normally does day to day. That's the point.

  Slow down.   Be present.

  Move your eyes in a different pattern.

  Reread.   Absorb.

  You may never come to enjoy the speed bumps, but you may grow to appreciate the gains you make as a result.

- Moving through *Intentional* offers options. The most straightforward approach is as a fifty-two-week journey, focusing on one choice per week. Meditate on the passage and questions for each choice daily as you create ways to practice it throughout the week. Notice what shifts and changes in your experience of the passage and questions each time you return to them after having practiced the choice in your life. Do this for five to six days with each choice, then give yourself one or two days off before advancing to the next choice. Your capacity to retain and utilize this work requires that you give your brain time to integrate what you've experienced, and that integration takes place during periods of rest, recovery, and play. So focus and practice for five or six days, then rest and play for one or two days. And repeat.

Regarding the questions, you may use them exactly as written or as a springboard that inspires other questions. You are free to take the questions in a different order from the one in which they are listed. Use the questions you find helpful and leave the ones you don't.

You might decide to pick the choice statement that calls to you each week rather than follow the choices in their listed order.

You could gather a group of friends and journey through *Intentional* together.

You may decide to use *Intentional* as an intensive personal retreat, initially working through the whole book over two or three days, then practicing your action, reflection, and integration over the weeks and months that follow.

Create your own unique approach to utilizing this work and move to the rhythm that suits you.

- But wait, there's more! For bonus material and companion resources to *Intentional*, visit:

<u>plenteouslife.com/Intentional</u>

Join the larger conversation—The Plenteous Life—from which *Intentional* was created. What is The Plenteous Life? I've included a brief introduction of The Plenteous Life at the end of this book in the Coming Work chapter to tell you more.

*Be in action
like your life depends on it,
because the life you desire
actually does.*

Foundations

Whether you are new to this adventure of intentionally creating your own way in the world or have been at it for some time, I'd like to share with you a context for *Intentional* that will serve you on your journey.

THE TRUTH

The real value of the work in front of you does not come from me having something new to *say* but from you having something new to *see* through your direct experimentation with each choice. I say this earnestly—I don't want you to believe anything I've written. Most of the time, belief is nothing more than mental acknowledgement of a concept and devoid of the corresponding action needed to actually make a difference in the quality of your life.

Again, do not believe me.

Nothing here is written to be right. Nothing here is written to be true. What I offer you with each choice is a new platform on which to stand and look at your life. From a new point of view, what do you see? Notice what's working, what's not working, and what else is possible for you.

Many of the choices,
and the things I say about them,
will land as gobbledygook to you.
And that is on purpose.

This book is not a social media post looking for "likes" and agreement. Anything that already makes sense to you, as well as anything that you already agree with, has no capacity to stretch you beyond who you already are. There is gold inside of you, and you will not access that treasure as long as you continue looking at your life in the same way as you have up until now.

This work is expressed
in a manner meant to get your attention
and help you uncover the gold
that has been buried inside of you for far too long.

It is intended to get under your skin
and into your life.

When the material disturbs or disrupts you in some way,
that is a great sign that you are striking gold.
So when an assertion hits a nerve,
keep digging.

Anytime you find yourself reacting to an assertion with some version of "I don't believe that," "That's not true," or "What about....," that's the sign that you're striking gold. In those moments, I'd like you to approach the disagreeable assertion as if you were trying on a new suit in the dressing room of a store or taking a new car for a test drive.

What do you notice about *yourself* in this moment?

Whether you agree with the assertion or not—buy it or not—is irrelevant with respect to seeing something new about your life as a result of trying it on.

Additional questions to help you try on disagreeable assertions:

- What about this assertion bothers me?
- With which of my beliefs does this assertion conflict?
- What about this assertion works for me?
- In what ways do I resist this assertion in my life?
- In what ways would this assertion serve me?
- In what ways would this assertion not serve me?
- What else is possible for me related to this assertion?

> The point of this entire book is to *see for yourself*
> something you've never seen before, and in so doing,
> access possibilities you've never had before.

So give yourself a break from the mental gymnastics of figuring out whether or not my words are true. Instead, use your direct experience with this material to discover and create a new possibility for your life.

FREEDOM

With every choice in this book, you are free to choose it and you are free to not choose it. You are free to act, and you are free to not act. You are free to say yes, and you are free to say no. There is no choice presented as a should, must, or ought. Every choice is simply *your* choice. Notice that when you fully own your freedom to choose, it produces an empowered experience with each choice.

When you abdicate your freedom to choose, it produces a disempowered experience with each choice. Ownership versus abdication—even that is your choice. You are the creator of your experience with *Intentional*.

WHEN CHOOSING SEEMS IMPOSSIBLE

Sometimes a presented choice may not look like something that can simply be chosen. Instead, it may look like an outcome rather than a choice that *produces* an outcome. The presented choice may also look like a situation outside of your direct control. How do you consciously choose an outcome or a situation outside of your direct control? Short answer: you choose it by choosing *how to see it*.

To unpack this idea, let's consider Viktor Frankl's premise that you are free to choose your attitude in "any given set of circumstances." He's really onto something here. The attitude Frankl is referring to is much more powerful than merely choosing to be happy when times are tough. No, to choose your attitude in any situation is to choose *how to see* the situation—to choose what the situation means to you, what you say about it, and ultimately what you decide is and isn't *possible, available,* and *accessible* for you in it.

How you see is both a filter and an activator playing a tremendous role in the quality of your life. Right now your brain is making thousands of how-to-see choices every minute that determine what you pay attention to and the meaning you make out of it. This process can be a wonderful strength or a horrible hindrance, depending on how your brain has been trained to interpret life. *How you see* is constant, continual, and predominantly unconscious.

People that regularly struggle to produce desirable outcomes usually do so because of an unconscious, unintentional how-to-see choice running undetected in their life—a choice to see their desired outcomes as *not* possible, *not* available, and *not* accessible. Until such a person becomes aware that this is the choice they are unintentionally making, it will never occur to them to choose otherwise.

Your freedom to choose your attitude means that in any given circumstance, you have the capacity to alter *how you see* your situation. So when in the course of this book it seems that the presented choice isn't possible to choose directly, you can choose to see it as *possible, available,* and *accessible* for you instead. This is a choice that will transform your experience with life.

Here are a couple of practical examples that demonstrate choosing *how to see* when choosing seems impossible:

Example 1: Imagine that you desire to lead a successful company, and you have struggled throughout your professional life to attain the magnitude of success you envision. In a situation like this, success won't look like something that you can choose directly. However, you *can* choose to see that attaining the success you desire is *possible, available,* and *accessible* for you even when the historical circumstances of your life suggest otherwise. The choice to see it as *possible, available,* and *accessible* will not only tune your awareness to the success you've attained already, it will also inform your follow-up choices and actions to produce success as a material result.

Example 2: Recall an experience you have had of great heartache or loss in a situation outside your control. When you look at that experience, do you see catastrophe or opportunity? Choosing to see opportunity as *possible, available,* and *accessible* for you, even in the midst of substantial heartache and loss, is the inalienable freedom you possess as a human being. It is the choice that will leverage every circumstance for your benefit.

So, the choice needed when it seems you have no choice is to *choose to see* the desired outcome as possible, available, and accessible for you. *Seeing* the outcome as possible, available, and accessible, in advance, precedes the way of *making* the outcome real as a result. Consciously choosing how you see a situation will empower you to identify new options of effective action for producing your desired result.

Don't take my word on this. Test it out for yourself and pay attention to what happens.

LANGUAGE

Throughout *Intentional* there are certain words and phrases that are used differently within the context of conscious choosing from how they are often used or defined in ordinary life. So to make sure we're on the same page, here is a brief glossary to reference as needed:

Come from: The state of being the source—the creator—of the *experience* one is having in every moment with their life circumstances, whether they recognize themselves to be the source or not.

Disempowerment: The state of not having access to the necessary power for acting effectively on behalf of oneself or another. It is often experienced as stuck-ness and helplessness.

Empowerment: The state of having access to the necessary power for acting effectively on behalf of oneself or another. It is often experienced as liberation and capableness.

Judgment: A determination that someone or something is good/bad, is right/wrong, or should/shouldn't be a particular way. Humans superimpose our personal judgment onto most situations. We then perceive the judgment to be inherent truth about the situation rather than a subjective condition we added to the situation.

Example: "Losing my job is bad, wrong, terrible, and shouldn't happen."

Meaning: An implication regarding someone's or something's past, present, or future derived from a judgment made about it. Human beings superimpose the meaning we've created onto most situations based on the judgment we've made. We then perceive the meaning to be inherent truth about the situation rather than a subjective condition we added to the situation.

Example: "Losing my job means I'll never be successful."

Resource: Anything that holds the potential to benefit, advance, or generate increase in one's life (e.g., time, money, energy, skill, talent, imagination, ambition, creativity, knowledge, vision, relationship, community).

Show up: The manner in which, through intention, perception, language, and action, one engages with life to generate a particular result. It is composed not only of how one presents oneself but also the way one perceives what is and isn't possible for themself or others in a particular moment.

VALUES

Whether you have identified them or not, core values are actively impacting the quality of your life right now. Core values are, simply, the things that are most important to you. Examples of core values are love, family, power, money, health, pleasure, fame, and freedom.

The quality of your life will increase or decrease in direct proportion to the alignment of your choices and core values. When your choices and values align, you'll experience your life working. When your choices and values misalign, you'll experience your life not working. It is incredibly useful, then, to get clear on what your core values are so that you can intentionally make choices consistent with what matters most to you.

GOD

Full disclosure: The pages in front of you rest upon the assertion that "God is." While *Intentional* is not a book about God, nor is it meant to change your view of God, it is biased toward the existence of God as the Creator, Giver, and Sustainer of life itself.

It is my assertion that the existence of God makes the human capacity for consciously choosing in life possible. It is also my assertion that there is power and support available to human beings that cannot be accessed through the physical or visible world alone; it must be accessed through the Spirit.

You do not need to subscribe to my assertions in order to be greatly served by *Intentional*. However, being informed of them may be useful to you as you choose how or whether to proceed with this work.

RESPONSIBILITY

Conscious choosing raises two fundamental questions that each of us gets to confront in life:

Who or what is responsible for how my life turns out?

And

Which choices do I make in light of who is responsible?

Who is responsible? Is it my parents, the government, my employer, my spouse, my friends, my skill and talent, the economy, my education, my circumstances, luck, the universe, or God? Am I responsible? And which choices in life are mine to make, if any?

Intentional will return you to wrestle with these two questions often. You're welcome.

PARADOX

The paradoxical nature of a deeply satisfying life is that if you treat it as a goal contingent upon external circumstances in the future, it will elude you. Deep satisfaction must come *from* you and *through* you in order to come *to* you. In other words, a deeply satisfying life is produced by being deeply satisfied. Hence, the paradox.

Deep satisfaction obeys the natural law of sowing and reaping; its nature is to come forth from your life like the multiplied return of cultivated seed. Choosing to be deeply satisfied *right now* is the seed that must be sown in to reap the deeply satisfying life you desire.

As with other paradoxes, the validity of this assertion becomes evident as you act on it rather than merely think about it. It is to be discovered through working it out, not figuring it out.

REPEAT

It will serve you greatly to revisit this section—Foundations—periodically as you progress through *Intentional*. Definitely do so anytime you experience yourself wrestling with concepts or ideas. It's also helpful to revisit from time to time to experience the Foundations principles at a deeper level as a result of who you have become along the way.

PROMISE

Some choices will generate immediate benefit, other choices will require persistent practice over weeks and months before you materialize the result you desire. My promise is that when you put this body of work into action, you will see new possibilities for your life. And when you see what you've never seen before, you will create what you've never created before.

Now is the time to consciously choose your own way.
Now is the time to bring forth something new.
Now is the time to create the deeply satisfying life you desire.

Now is the time to be *Intentional.*

52 MAXIMS OF
Conscious Choosing

WEEK 1

01

I choose to...

Act
Now

The life you desire can only be created now.
Not someday, not even tomorrow; those don't
exist in the realm of direct experience.
Have you ever done anything tomorrow? No!
Anything you have ever done has always and
only ever been done right now. Notice that.
There is no future in the realm of direct experience.
What you call the future is actually your next right now.
And how you spend *this* right now
is how you spend *every* right now.
How are you spending right now? Preparing and waiting
for life to begin one day after certain conditions are met?
Or are you living fully now, loving without restraint now,
taking action now?
Now is the only time you ever will.

Experiment • Discover

Have you ever done anything tomorrow?

NEW PERSPECTIVE AND POSSIBILITY

- What is something important that I've been putting off until I'm "ready"?

- What is delay costing me?

- When I choose to live now, rather than to perpetually get ready to live, what action becomes available to me?

Practice • Grow

WEEK 2

02

I choose to...

Own My
Choices

As a human being, you can easily have the experience
that life is happening to you. You can just as easily have
the experience that you are actively participating
as co-creator with life. What makes the difference
between these two experiences is the degree to
which you acknowledge that the conditions of your
life come primarily from the choices you make.
Even when life is so hard that the only choice you
can acknowledge is that you choose to wake up and
stay on the planet one more day, you can own it
and be responsible for it.
Most choices happen so subtly that they give you the
impression of not having been chosen at all. If you slow
down and notice just how many choices you actually
make moment by moment, you will experience how
free you really are...even in the midst of others' choices
that have real impact on you.
Ownership has privileges; with it come power and peace
to keep creating your life in the face of any circumstance.
In contrast, abdicating ownership of your choices
cuts off access to that power and peace,
leaving you helpless in every circumstance.
What's really at stake is not *what* you choose
but that you *own* the choosing of it.

Experiment • Discover

> Ownership has privileges; with it come power and peace to keep creating your life in the face of any circumstance.

NEW PERSPECTIVE AND POSSIBILITY

- In my experience, is life happening to me, or am I actively co-creating with life?

- What choices have I made over the past twenty-four hours?

- What choices have I made that have produced the current conditions of my life?

- What possibilities become available to me as I fully own the choices I've made so far?

- What do I choose now?

Practice • Grow

WEEK 3

03

I choose to...

Create

In life, you don't get what you want;
you get what you create.
And you create your life through the focus and mastery
of your thoughts, emotions, words, and actions.
You always get what you create.
If anything is missing from your life,
it's only because you have not yet created it...
and that's really great news!
Stop wishing, hoping, begging, or longing for what
you desire; that serves only to distract you
from the one thing that would make the
difference for you: *creating* what you desire.
Eating eliminates hunger, and creating eliminates want.
You will never be stopped by current circumstances when
you develop your capacity to create new circumstances.

Experiment • Discover

If anything is missing from your
life, it's only because
you have not yet created it...
and that's really great news!

NEW PERSPECTIVE AND POSSIBILITY

- What are some differences between wanting and creating?

- What's missing from my life?

- Who must I be to create what's missing?

- What action will I take to create what's missing?

- If I don't yet know how to create what I desire, what action will I take to learn?

Practice • Grow

WEEK 4

I choose to...

Leverage
Adversity

Consider that in every adversity, life is delivering to
you a resource that you wouldn't have otherwise.
This resource is your advantage.
But the advantage won't be obvious
to your natural eye—it will be raw,
rough, immature, and likely covered in shit.
It is the raw material out of which
skills, character, ideas, connections, perceptions,
capabilities, and opportunities are forged.
Your work is to see with the eye of possibility,
to recognize this raw material as a resource
with which you can make something useful. If you choose,
you can leverage every adversity to your advantage.
Remember:
1) You don't step into greatness *in spite* of the challenge;
you step into greatness *because* of the challenge.
And:
2) Shit is incredibly valuable; it helps things grow.

Experiment • Discover

You don't step into greatness
in spite of the challenge;
you step into greatness
because of the challenge.

NEW PERSPECTIVE AND POSSIBILITY

- What adversity have I experienced?

- What gifts, lessons, and benefits has life given me through difficulty?

- What can I create out of adversity?

- How will I leverage adversity to advance my life?

- How can the pain I've experienced be of service to others?

Practice • Grow

WEEK 5

I choose to...

Be
Curious

I have found that the best antidote to
judgment, cynicism, irritation, condemnation,
misunderstanding, fear, and boredom is curiosity.
Curiosity is a place of discovery, invention, and awe that
instantly transforms the mundane into adventure.
It is a doorway to new possibility.
Curiosity will cause you to see and hear things
you were blind and deaf to moments before.
Imagine the quality of your life when curiosity—the
discovery, invention, and awe of new possibility—is
your normal way of moving through the world.

Experiment • Discover

Curiosity is a doorway to new possibility.

NEW PERSPECTIVE AND POSSIBILITY

- Where do I experience awe and mystery?

- What do I notice—what do I experience—when I bring curiosity rather than judgment to people or situations I don't like?

- What happens when I approach my day as if I know nothing about anything?

- What questions will I generate to discover new depths and dimensions in people, places, ideas, and things?

Practice • Grow

WEEK 6

06

I choose to...
Unlearn

Your current results in life are coming from your current
habits, patterns, expectations, perceived limitations,
skills, thinking, speaking, and way of seeing the world.
It's all been learned.
Much of your learning didn't even originate with you.
You inherited it from the people and places
that formed your experiences growing up.
Previous learning isn't inherently true or false;
it's just familiar and well established.
It takes up precious room in your brain,
dictating what is and isn't possible for you right now.
When generating new results,
not only will there be things to learn,
but there will also be things to *unlearn*.
To unlearn is to consciously stop the autopilot programs
of previous learning to create space
for new learning to take hold;
it is similar to pulling weeds in a garden.
There are things you desire for your life now that
will not flourish until you weed out or eliminate
certain habits and patterns.
It will serve you greatly to unlearn any previous learning
that conflicts with your new desires.

Experiment • Discover

Previous learning isn't
inherently true or false;
it's just familiar and well established. It
takes up precious room in your brain,
dictating what is and isn't possible for
you right now.

NEW PERSPECTIVE AND POSSIBILITY

- What habitual thinking, speaking, actions, and perceived limitations have I inherited from others? What difference will it make for me to unlearn them?

- What patterns have I learned that are no longer serving me? What new choices would help me to unlearn them?

- What do I want for myself now that's in conflict with what I previously learned is and isn't possible for me?

Practice • Grow

WEEK 7

07

I choose to...

Think
New
Thoughts

By the time you reach adulthood, a majority of your thoughts each day are a repeat of the thoughts you had the day before. There is nothing wrong with this. In fact, repetition is quite helpful for your daily functioning. Your brain is designed to economize energy. It takes much less energy to repeat and reinforce the thought patterns that already exist than to generate and establish new ones. So your default thinking—the way you think without intentionally thinking otherwise—will always pull toward repetition; it has no capacity for newness. Here's why thinking matters so much when it comes to the quality of your life: Your thoughts generate your actions that generate your conditions. Take a look at the current conditions of your life; they originated from the dominate thoughts you've had up until now. To the degree your current conditions are as you'd like them to be, your dominant thoughts are serving you. To the degree your current conditions are not as you'd like them to be, your dominant thoughts are not serving you. The thoughts that originated your current conditions have no power to create new conditions. Therefore, you will not create *new* conditions as long you repetitively think the thoughts that created your *current* conditions. Generating new conditions, then, starts with generating new thoughts.

Experiment • Discover

Your thoughts generate your actions that generate your conditions. Generating new conditions, then, starts with generating new thoughts.

NEW PERSPECTIVE AND POSSIBILITY

- What is the impact of my current thinking on the quality of my life?

- Which of my dominant thoughts are no longer serving me?

- Based on the new experiences I now desire, what new thoughts will it take to generate them?

Practice • Grow

WEEK 8

I choose to...

Be
Loved

You don't deserve love.
And you will never deserve love,
because love is not something to be deserved;
love is something for which you are designed.
You probably don't impose a requirement
of deservedness for other things you're designed for,
such as air and water. How silly would this be:
"I don't deserve air. I haven't earned it."
"I don't deserve water. I'm not worthy of it."
You are designed for air; you are designed for water.
And you are designed for love.
Love is; you are made of it, from it, and for it.
You are surrounded by it.
You are designed to love and be loved.
All attempts to *deserve* love serve only to prevent you
from experiencing that you *are* love.
You can either experience love or shut yourself off to it,
but deserving love is something you will never, ever do.
I hope that lands for you as something to celebrate.

Experiment • Discover

All attempts to *deserve* love
serve only to prevent you
from experiencing that
you *are* love.

NEW PERSPECTIVE AND POSSIBILITY

- In what ways do I welcome love in my life?

- In what ways do I shut myself off from love?

- What do my current circumstances suggest about my openness to love?

- When I see myself *as* love, how does that change my everyday experience?

Practice • Grow

WEEK 9

09

I choose to...

Heal

Your natural state as a human being
is complete well-being
in body, mind, and soul.
Who you are already, at your core, is well.
You are designed in such a way that when a wounding
takes place, your natural default is to heal.
When healing doesn't occur, it's because
a toxin is present, interfering with recovery.
Toxins come in many forms,
such as fear, rage, unforgiveness,
bitterness, and resentment.
Your work is to rid yourself of the toxin;
your body, mind, and soul will handle the repair.
And should you find yourself resisting the work of
ridding the toxin, then you're likely dealing with hidden
benefits of maintaining the wound. Hidden benefits
are very, very expensive—they keep you from the
life you would otherwise have without them.
Once you become aware of how exactly
hidden benefits are costing you,
you can consciously decide
whether to keep paying that price or not.

Experiment • Discover

Your work is to rid yourself
of the toxin;
your body,
mind,
and soul
will handle the repair.

NEW PERSPECTIVE AND POSSIBILITY

- What wound have I ignored or buried?

- What wound have I not let heal?

- How is the pain from this wound impacting my life?

- What benefits do I get from maintaining this wound?

- What becomes available to me when this wound heals?

Practice • Grow

WEEK 10

I choose to...

Cultivate Joy

You will never get happy.
Happiness is not a place to get to;
it's a place to come from.
No circumstance can *make* you happy.
Happiness is intentionally created within you,
like a crop in a field.
It is chosen, planted, nurtured, and ruthlessly protected.
When you see yourself to be a joy maker,
you'll stop trying to get joy *from* your circumstance
and instead bring the joy you have already produced
to your circumstance.

Experiment • Discover

Happiness is not a place to get to; it's a place to come from.

NEW PERSPECTIVE AND POSSIBILITY

- Where do I focus my attention that depletes my joy?

- What practices of mine cultivate and produce happiness?

- In what ways will I bring joy to my work, home, and community?

- What does it take for me to protect joy?

- How does coming from happiness impact my day-to-day experience?

Practice • Grow

WEEK 11

I choose to...

Clear the
Clutter

Life shows up in the space created for it.
Most people, rather than actively clearing space,
are habitually accumulating instead.
We wind up cluttered in our minds, relationships,
commitments, and surroundings because we don't
intentionally purge, say no, set boundaries,
and eliminate the things that no longer serve us.
The nature of the space you make will determine
what gets in and what stays out,
what flourishes and what diminishes in your life.

Experiment • Discover

Life shows up
in the space
created for it.

NEW PERSPECTIVE AND POSSIBILITY

- What spaces, experiences, or situations were valuable or useful at one time that are no longer serving me?

- What new spaces, experiences, or situations would serve the person I am becoming?

- What am I making room for in my life?

- What am I not making room for in my life?

Practice • Grow

WEEK 12

I choose to...
Acknowledge
My Strength

You

are

more

powerful

than you know.

If you could get a glimpse of how much so,

it would leave you speechless.

Know that your way of being calls forth being in others.

When you play small, you call forth smallness in others.

When you stand in your greatness,

you call forth greatness in others.

When you acknowledge your strength,

you call forth strength in others.

Who you are for yourself is who others get to be with you.

Do you realize the impact you have,

just from who you are?

Imagine owning your power unapologetically.

What would be possible for you then?

Experiment • Discover

When you stand in your greatness,
you call forth greatness in others.
When you acknowledge your strength,
you call forth strength in others.

NEW PERSPECTIVE AND POSSIBILITY

- What do I like about myself? What am I great at?

- What character traits do I possess that have been forged through fire?

- What strengths have I dismissed or failed to acknowledge?

- In what ways have I grown this past year?

- How does it feel to acknowledge that I am powerful?

Practice • Grow

WEEK 13

13

I choose to...

Convert Fear into Fuel

Human beings are born with two innate fears:
loud noise and physically falling.
All other fear is learned.
Every fear you have right now, minus loud noises
and falling, was learned at some point in your life.
Even the way you *relate* to fear—
what you do with it—was learned.
Do you use fear as a reason to stop? You have learned to
be fear's slave. Do you use fear as fuel to press onward?
You have learned to be fear's master.
Fear is energy;
it is power at your disposal.
Fear will absolutely serve you...
the moment you choose that it does so.
So put fear to work.
The sooner you channel fear into action,
the sooner you'll advance your life.

Experiment • Discover

Fear is energy; it is power at your disposal.

NEW PERSPECTIVE AND POSSIBILITY

- Which of my desires are currently being impacted by fear?

- How can I use fear energy to advance those desires instead of using fear as a reason to stop?

- What step of action will I take today?

Practice • Grow

WEEK 14

I choose to...

See That I Matter

Whether you realize it or not,
you have a relationship with yourself,
a way of seeing yourself.
And in this relationship, it is very common to question
whether or not you matter. It's also common to
look to your accomplishments and recognitions
as proof for or against yourself.
Have you ever considered that the very attempt to validate
that you matter is perpetuating your sense that you don't?
I invite you to use a different criterion for
determining whether you matter or not.
I don't claim this criterion to be *the truth*,
and if you try it on, I say you'll experience a
breakthrough in your relationship with yourself.
You matter because of one thing and one thing alone...
you are here.
Your being here is the only evidence
you will ever have to see that you matter.
That's it.
No other proof can settle this once and for all for you.
All other attempts to validate yourself
are just a waste of your precious time and energy.
You are here, therefore you matter.
So show up in your life
like you make a difference in how it turns out,
because as long as you're here,
you actually do.

Experiment • Discover

Show up in your life like you make
a difference in how it turns out,
because as long as you're here,
you actually do.

NEW PERSPECTIVE AND POSSIBILITY

- What becomes possible for me when I see that I matter simply because I am here?

- What impact does my presence make on others?

- In what ways do I live as though my life doesn't count?

- How will I show up at work, home, and community as an expression that I matter?

- What contribution will I make today?

- In what ways can I show up for me?

Practice • Grow

WEEK 15

I choose to...

Know What I Want

There is a secret upside to staying confused
or unclear about what you want in life:
it lets you off the hook for being responsible
to create something that actually matters to you.
It's amazing how many people
will sacrifice what they really want
in order to avoid being responsible
for how their life turns out.
On the other hand, when you know what you want
and are truly committed to your desired result,
you'll find a way to create it.

Experiment • Discover

When you know what you want
and are truly committed
to your desired result,
you'll find a way to create it.

NEW PERSPECTIVE AND POSSIBILITY

- What hidden benefits do I get by being indecisive or confused about what I want?

- What does it cost me to stay unclear about what I want?

- What do I truly desire in each area of my life?

- What is it about each of my desires that makes it important to me?

Practice • Grow

WEEK 16

16

I choose to...

Decide

The word *decide* means to cut away, kill off,
or strike down options. It shares a Latin root with
homi*cide,* geno*cide,* and pesti*cide.* A decision
focuses your energy in a particular direction,
which powerfully advances your life.
So why do you delay decisions?
One of the biggest reasons you delay
decisions is that your future looks to you
to be uncertain and unpredictable:
"I can't decide today because
I don't know what will happen tomorrow.
What if my circumstances change?
What if I change my mind?
What if I can't handle it?
What if I fail?"
And that's the disempowered trap that will have you
delay your life away.
Here's the way out of the trap:
be the certainty you are waiting for.
Be responsible for creating the future you desire
like it really does depend on you.
Show up in your work, relationships, and health
like you make a difference
in how they turn out—because you do.
You'll have no need to delay decisions
when you get fully responsible for the outcome.

Experiment • Discover

Be the certainty you're waiting for.
Be responsible
for creating the future you desire
like it really does depend on you.

NEW PERSPECTIVE AND POSSIBILITY

- What decision for my life have I been delaying?

- What options am I considering that need to be cut off?

- In what ways will deciding benefit me?

- What decisive action will I take when I get fully responsible for the outcome?

Practice • Grow

WEEK 17

I choose to...

Make Bold Requests

People refrain from being bold
because they're more concerned
with what others may think of them
than they are concerned
with getting what they actually want.
Rather than go after a life that would light them up,
most people resign themselves to tolerating a life
that they are too timid to do anything about.
Being bold is risky
and
not nearly as risky as being timid.
Between the two, being bold is much more likely
to produce the life you desire.

Experiment • Discover

Being bold is risky
and
not nearly as risky as being timid.

NEW PERSPECTIVE AND POSSIBILITY

- Where do I hesitate in going for what I really want?

- What's at risk when I'm timid?

- What and how do I feel when I'm bold?

- How do I feel when I get what I actually want?

- What's at risk when I'm bold?

- What's one bold request or action I will make for each area of life that matters to me?

Practice • Grow

WEEK 18

I choose to...
Deal with What's Not Working

To be human is to create.
You cannot *not* create; it's in your DNA.
Both consciously and unconsciously,
you create your life through the choices you make.
In every moment, with every choice,
you are either creating the life you want
or the life you don't want.
Avoiding or tolerating unworkable behaviors
and situations—with yourself and with others—
is a great way to create the life you don't want.
Deal with what's not working in your life
or be left to deal with a life that doesn't work.
It will cost you something to deal with that unworkability.
And it will cost immeasurably more if you don't.

Experiment • Discover

Deal with what's not working in your life
or be left to deal
with a life that doesn't work.

NEW PERSPECTIVE AND POSSIBILITY

- What's not working in my life?

- What choices have I made that created the current unworkability?

- What choices could I make to have my life work?

Practice • Grow

WEEK 19

I choose to...

Stop Looking
and
Start Seeing

Looking for something and seeing something
are not the same experience.
As long as you're looking, you're not seeing.
The moment you see, you stop looking.
Looking for opportunity everywhere is a very different
experience from *seeing* opportunity everywhere.
Notice that.
You always interact with your situation in a
manner consistent with how you see it,
so it will serve you to see your situation in a manner
consistent with the experience you wish to have.
Vividly engage your imagination.
Seeing your desires as available and easy to attain
allows you to experience them
as available and easy to attain.

Experiment • Discover

Looking for opportunity everywhere
is a very different experience from
seeing opportunity everywhere.

NEW PERSPECTIVE AND POSSIBILITY

- What have I been looking for that continues to elude me?

- What favorable conditions will I see myself as being surrounded by?

- How might I vividly imagine my desired outcome to see it as easy to attain?

Practice • Grow

WEEK 20

I choose to...

Play and Laugh

Play and laughter come naturally to us as children,
but we often learn that growing up means
growing serious and somber
as a necessary approach to adult life.
Play and laughter are seen as the fantasies of childhood
and not useful for the harsh realities of adulthood.
Consider that play and laughter
come naturally to us when we are young
not because we are *children* but because we are *human*.
I say one of the most mature things an adult can do
is approach each day from play and laughter;
and on the hard days, double it.
In the darkest of times,
in the most difficult of situations,
play and laughter are reservoirs of
great strength and vitality.
Play and laughter heal us,
energize us,
sustain us,
and renew us.
And the wise among us employ them generously.

Experiment • Discover

Play and laughter come naturally
to us when we are young
not because we are *children*
but because we are *human*.

NEW PERSPECTIVE AND POSSIBILITY

- When was the last time I laughed so hard that I cried or peed my pants?

- How do I need to look at life so I experience it as play?

- Where can I intentionally see humor in everyday life?

- How will I generate play and laughter today?

Practice • Grow

WEEK 21

I choose to...

Connect

You are made for connection.
Authentic connection with other living beings deepens
and expands your experience in life,
even the experience you have with yourself.
Actively cultivate your relationships.
Practice the art of presence,
being fully engaged and attentive in every interaction.
Initiate meaningful conversations that require
vulnerability. Seek diverse perspectives and embrace
differences.
Invest in individuals who inspire and challenge you,
as it is in their presence that you access untapped
potential,
unlock doors to unexpected opportunities,
and accelerate your growth.
These are the courageous acts that forge authentic
connection. Through them, you will discover the deep
richness of every moment and expand
beyond your current limitations.
It is through connection that the fullness
of all you are capable of becoming is realized,
surpassing all you could ever be on your own.

Experiment • Discover

Authentic connection with
other living beings
deepens and expands your
experience in life.

NEW PERSPECTIVE AND POSSIBILITY

- By whom am I deeply known and seen?

- What will connection require of me?

- What is currently missing in my life that connection would provide?

- In what ways can I increase connection physically, emotionally, intellectually, socially, and spiritually?

- What common ground will I generate with those whom I view as different from me?

Practice • Grow

WEEK 22

I choose to...
Be
Responsible

Responsibility is literally the ability to respond.
It is power and freedom to create in every circumstance.
Always.
In every way that you are willing to be responsible,
you access power to deal effectively with your life.
Being responsible for the outcome of every situation
that matters to you, whether you are at fault for its
current condition or not, is the only way to create
anything new.
You can either be a victim or be responsible.
Put responsibility to the test and watch your life
transform.

Experiment • Discover

Responsibility
is power and freedom
to create in every circumstance.
Always.

NEW PERSPECTIVE AND POSSIBILITY

- In what ways can I be responsible even when I am not to blame or at fault?

- How will my life change if I take full responsibility for how it turns out?

- How will I show up differently at work and home as being responsible for the experiences created there?

Practice • Grow

WEEK 23

I choose to...

Do...
or Do Not

Stop trying—it doesn't work.
Trying is a concept that exists in language
but not in the realm of direct experience.
In direct experience, there is doing and not doing.
As long as you are trying, you are *not* doing,
while deceiving yourself that you *are* doing.
Trying is a socially acceptable way
to feel better about not doing,
and it will leave you disempowered and exhausted.
Doing works. Not doing works.
But trying—not doing while deceiving yourself
that you are doing—doesn't work.

Experiment • Discover

Trying is a socially acceptable way
to feel better about not doing.
Doing works.
Not doing works.
But trying doesn't work.

NEW PERSPECTIVE AND POSSIBILITY

- What will I do this day?

- What will I not do this day?

- What disempowered judgments do I make regarding doing and not doing?

- What's my experience with life when I stop making doing and not doing good or bad, right or wrong?

Practice • Grow

WEEK 24

I choose to...
Get
Uncomfortable

Most people avoid discomfort.
This is unfortunate because discomfort correlates with
growth. In fact, your life will grow in direct proportion
to the uncomfortable actions you take.
A choice for comfort will cost your growth;
a choice for growth will cost your comfort.
If you're committed to growth,
you must stop using discomfort as your signal to retreat
and start using it as your signal to advance.
Rather than avoid discomfort, seek it out, pursue it.
Celebrate discomfort;
it means you're growing.

Experiment • Discover

A choice for comfort
will cost your growth;
a choice for growth
will cost your comfort.

NEW PERSPECTIVE AND POSSIBILITY

- In what ways do I intentionally seek out discomfort?

- What do I do when I am uncomfortable?

- What is something I deeply desire that is only accessible outside my current comfort zone?

- Am I willing to look foolish, be wrong, make mistakes, not know, feel pain, and face fear in order to grow?

Practice • Grow

WEEK 25

I choose to...

Honor
My Word

Your life will work, or not,
to the degree you keep and honor your word.
Your word in corresponding action is integrity.
Where integrity increases,
so does the workability and quality of your life.
Where integrity decreases,
so does the workability and quality of your life.
Whether you realize it or not, your very sense of who
you are and what you can count on yourself for will either
expand or erode in direct proportion to the integrity
of your word and action.
In every moment, when it comes to doing
what you say you will do,
your choice is to either honor your ever-shifting moods,
thoughts, feelings, and circumstances
or to honor your word.

Experiment • Discover

Your very sense of who you are
and what you can count on yourself for
will either expand or erode
in direct proportion to the integrity
of your word and action.

NEW PERSPECTIVE AND POSSIBILITY

- What is my word worth to myself and others?

- What's the impact of keeping my word?

- What's the impact of *not* keeping my word?

- What will change in my life as I increase fulfilling my promises and agreements?

- How would I behave if I put $50,000 on the line every time I gave my word?

Practice • Grow

WEEK 26

I choose to...

Be
Clear

It takes real work to be clear—
clear about who you are, your purpose, what you want,
your life direction, what you ask for, who you serve,
what you offer, what you value, etc.
Getting clear will cost you, and that cost is insanely
cheap compared to the cost of lingering in confusion and
ambiguity. Confusion and ambiguity will drain you of
resources
and leave you running in circles.
Murky seasons are sure to come,
but perpetually remaining in darkness is a subconscious
choice to stay in your comfort zone
rather than to be responsible for how your life turns out.
Once you are clear, decisions get easy.
All of your energy previously spent on vacillating between
options gets focused into propelling your life forward.
Being clear is essential to being unstoppable
in creating a life you love.

Experiment • Discover

Getting clear will cost you,
and that cost is insanely cheap
compared to the cost of lingering
in confusion and ambiguity.

NEW PERSPECTIVE AND POSSIBILITY

- In what areas of life am I struggling due to confusion or ambiguity?

- What stops me from being clear?

- What hidden benefits do I get from not getting clear?

- When I am clear, what actions and benefits become available to me as a result?

- What changes must I make in my environment, relationships, behaviors, and choices to create clarity for myself?

Practice • Grow

WEEK 27

I choose to...
Grow

There's no magic formula for growth.
Will a certain method help? Test it out, experiment;
see what works and what doesn't.
Growth is less about getting it right and more about
getting present to what happens in you each time you
experiment.
Getting present means being aware of what's useful
and what no longer serves you in life.
Pay attention to what produces
your desired results and what doesn't.
What helps you grow today
may actually hinder tomorrow.
Relying on a formula or tactic that worked in the past
is just more of being not present
to what is and isn't happening for you right now.
So give it a go, notice, adjust. Do it again.
And by all means, have some fun doing it,
because happiness is a byproduct of growth.

Experiment • Discover

Growth is less about getting it right and more about getting present to what happens in you.

NEW PERSPECTIVE AND POSSIBILITY

- When was the last time a person, idea, activity, or situation challenged me into great growth? What changed as a result?

- What's something new I will take on today?

- What glorious blunder did I make today (or in the past), and what did I learn?

- When I'm growing, what's happening and not happening in my life?

Practice • Grow

WEEK 28

I choose to...
Experiment

When life is approached as an exam
the focus is on getting it right and not getting it wrong.
It's marked by fear, stress, and tension. Getting it
wrong in an exam often means failure, defeat, and
discouragement.
When life is approached as an experiment,
the focus is on discovering what does and doesn't work.
It's marked by exploration, fascination, and wonder.
Getting it wrong in an experiment
is really a discovery of what doesn't work,
and encouragement to explore another way instead.
Notice the difference in results:
Your life can be very right and still very unworkable.
When your life works, being right no longer matters.

Experiment • Discover

Your life can be very right
and still very unworkable.
When your life works,
being right no longer matters.

NEW PERSPECTIVE AND POSSIBILITY

- Do I see life as an experiment to discover or as an exam to get right?

- What do I risk when I approach life as an exam?

- What do I risk when I approach life as an experiment?

- What's working and not working in my life?

- What am I learning?

Practice • Grow

WEEK 29

I choose to...

Develop
My Body

Life in this world needs a vehicle
through which it can express itself.
For you, that vehicle is the human body.
It is through your body that you as a conscious soul
express yourself as distinctly human. Your body is not a
separate, independent unit from the rest of you.
It is inextricably interconnected and interdependent
with the whole of your being for as long as you walk
the earth.
In an age where it is common to develop the intellect
while disregarding the body,
you will do yourself a great favor
by investing in your physical well-being.
The health of your body materially affects the
quality of your thoughts and emotions, your range of
communication, your available energy, and your overall
capacity to create.
Much like a motor vehicle, the condition of your body
impacts not only where you can go in life
but how you get there.
You will more easily, more effectively, and more enjoyably
create more of what you desire
when your vehicle—your body—is optimized
to support you.

Experiment • Discover

> Your body is inextricably interconnected and interdependent with the whole of your being.

NEW PERSPECTIVE AND POSSIBILITY

- How is my current physical condition impacting the quality of my life?

- What does my body need for me to start doing?

- What does my body need for me to stop doing?

- What physical activities do I enjoy most?

- What disempowered beliefs about my body am I willing to let go?

- In what ways must I develop physically in order to produce the life I desire more effectively?

Practice • Grow

WEEK 30

30

I choose to...

Feed My
Imagination

One of the greatest things about your imagination
is that it is not limited by your current reality.
Imagination is the blueprint of your coming reality.
Imagination is *your* instruction to *your* subconscious
brain regarding the future experiences
you will live into.
It inspires the emotion *you* feel
and the action *you* take
to make the invisible visible.
Whatever you imagine vividly and regularly
—with corresponding emotion and action—
will materialize eventually.

Experiment • Discover

Whatever you imagine vividly
and regularly
—with corresponding emotion
and action—
will materialize eventually.

NEW PERSPECTIVE AND POSSIBILITY

- What do I think about most of the time?

- What activities, places, and people light me up and get me seeing new possibilities?

- What activities, places, and people stifle my imagination?

- Where on my calendar is "feed my imagination" scheduled?

Practice • Grow

WEEK 31

31

I choose to...
Actualize My Purpose

For conscious souls, mere existence is excruciating.
We are imbued with the will to live for much more than
survival.
People are made for purpose.
When we live without a sense of purpose,
we fail to use our creative power
as a contribution in the world.
Without purpose, we abuse ourselves and others,
devolving into distraction, destruction, and despair.
Whatever you do, actualize your purpose.
Discover it.
Generate it.
Decide it.
Choose it.
Develop it.
Live from it.
Purpose is the deep satisfaction
every conscious soul craves.
It is inspiration, energy, and direction.
It will fortify you, guarding and guiding you
through the uncertainties of life.
Purpose will liberate you from the drudgery
of survival existence, elevating your vision beyond yourself
and maturing you into the co-creator with life
you are designed to be.
Remember, you are a creator-being. As such, your purpose
will always include some form of creating, producing,
and contributing as an expression of who you are.

Experiment • Discover

Whatever you do,
actualize your purpose.
Discover it. Generate it.
Decide it. Choose it. Develop it.
Live from it.

NEW PERSPECTIVE AND POSSIBILITY

- What do I choose now?

- What is it that I live for? What is my compelling "why"?

- In what ways will I create my day as an expression of purpose?

- Where do I experience fulfillment and meaning in life?

- What am I here to give?

Practice • Grow

WEEK 32

I choose to...

Be
Still

Every living thing is pulsating and cycling
between states of on and off.
It is this alternation of on and off that creates
usefulness and beauty.
Motion requires rest, focus requires diffusion, sound
requires silence, awake requires asleep.
And productivity requires stillness.
In stillness you recover, repair, refuel,
recharge, release, and reset.
Stillness returns you to who you really are.
The natural state of water is clear. When water is murky,
the simplest way to clean it is to leave it alone,
to let it *be still.*
In stillness, everything that is not water separates away
and settles to the bottom, leaving the water effortlessly
restored
to its natural clear state.
Similarly, the natural state
of a human being— your natural state—is well.
When you find yourself experiencing something other
than wellness in life, the simplest,
most direct path back to it is stillness.
Your stillness returns you to your wellness.
Are you exhausted? Confused?
Have you lost your joy? Your edge?
Be still.

Experiment • Discover

Your stillness returns you to your wellness.

NEW PERSPECTIVE AND POSSIBILITY

- What do I experience when I practice stillness?

- What does it look like to be still in the midst of activity?

- How might my stillness be of service to others?

- When was the last time I took a full day off to rest?

- How will I practice stillness daily, weekly, monthly, and annually?

Practice • Grow

WEEK 33

I choose to...

Be Kind

There is a lower self and higher self in each of us.
The lower self is expressed in the excuses,
reasons, mediocrity, and fear
that a person uses to justify playing small in life.
The higher self is expressed in the creativity, possibility,
power, and courage that a person uses to actualize
who they are capable of being in life.
In every moment, you are serving either
the lower self or the higher self
in yourself and others.
Which self you are serving depends on
an important distinction:
Are you being nice or being kind?
In everyday language, nice and kind are used
interchangeably, but niceness and kindness come from
different motivations
and produce very different results.
Niceness holds back the truth when the truth is difficult to
say or do. It is a covert way to avoid *your* discomfort at the
possibility of others getting upset. In the name of sparing
others' feelings, you're actually sparing your own and lying
to yourself about it. To prioritize your comfort over the
highest good of others is to serve the lower self.
In contrast, kindness is forthright with the truth,
even when the truth is difficult to say or do.
It is a stand for how powerful others actually are
and the greatness they are capable of in life,
regardless of whether they get upset
or you get uncomfortable.
To prioritize the highest good of others over your comfort
is to serve the higher self.

Experiment • Discover

Kindness is a stand for how powerful others actually are and the greatness they are capable of in life.

NEW PERSPECTIVE AND POSSIBILITY

- How would being kind rather than nice impact my life?

- What kindness is missing from my home, work, or community, and how will I provide it?

- What happens in me when I am kind to others?

- What's the most uncomfortable kind thing someone has said or done to me that served my highest good?

Practice • Grow

WEEK 34

34

I choose to...

Serve

I think Jesus was letting us in on one of the greatest
secrets
to life when he said he came to
serve
rather than to be served.
Your task is to discover how you enjoy serving
and whom you enjoy serving.
Discovery will not come through *figuring* this out
but through *working* this out,
because the idea of service and the act of service
are two vastly different things.
It is through the direct experience of service that you'll
discover who and what lights you up and,
just as importantly, who and what does not.
So get in motion with service:
serve different kinds of people in different kinds of ways.
As you discover how and whom you enjoy serving,
your service to others will become deeply satisfying
and energizing for you.

Experiment • Discover

As you discover how and whom
you enjoy serving,
your service to others will become
deeply satisfying
and energizing for you.

NEW PERSPECTIVE AND POSSIBILITY

- Who am I serving through my life?

- What value do I produce for others?

- What do I experience when I serve others?

- In which ways do I enjoy serving?

- How can I create a fabulous life through service?

Practice • Grow

WEEK 35

35

I choose to...

Hold
Nothing
Back

"Playing it safe" isn't actually safe.
While safety may keep you from failure and death
—for a while—
it will keep you from full aliveness as well.
Plants don't produce fruit when in a state of self-
protection, and neither does your life.
Getting ready to live "one day" or "someday" isn't really
living. As long as you are getting ready to live *one* day,
you are not living right *now*.
And now is the only time you have.

Experiment • Discover

As long as you are
getting ready to live *one* day,
you are not living right *now*.

NEW PERSPECTIVE AND POSSIBILITY

- What does full aliveness mean to me?

- Where and how do I hold back?

- What must change in order to bring my full self to every area of my life that matters to me?

- What do I look like fully alive?

- Who do I know living fully right now?

Practice • Grow

WEEK 36

36

I choose to...

Make a Difference for Others

Life takes on great purpose once you see that
who you are
is
contribution.
You ARE contribution.
Consider the difference you make every time you choose
to show up as contribution in your home, school, work,
and community. You bring things and experiences into
the world that would not have existed without you.
I want you to get that who you really are
is significant
and powerful
and more than enough.
It's time to experience yourself this way.
The world needs you to live this out.
Every. Day.

Experiment • Discover

You ARE contribution.

NEW PERSPECTIVE AND POSSIBILITY

- What does being contribution mean for me?

- How will I use my power to empower others?

- What impact will I make today?

- With what act of kindness could I surprise someone?

- What experiences are waiting on me to create them?

Practice • Grow

WEEK 37

37

I choose to...

Commit

There is a difference between
the concept of commitment
and the experience of commitment.
As a concept, commitment may appear as restrictive,
daunting, or oppressive. It is often characterized as a "should,"
an "ought to," the right thing,
an obligation, or even a prison.
But the experience of commitment, of sincerely committing
yourself to a particular outcome or result,
is one of being moved into action.
Commitment is desire in motion.
I can show you exactly what you are and are not committed to
by the action you are and are not taking.
Without action, your desire may be many things—a wish,
hope, want, fantasy, or longing—but it is not commitment.
And it really is that simple.
Without commitment, nothing changes.
With commitment, miracles unfold.
The experience of commitment is resolute steadfastness to
keep at it until you complete what you set out to accomplish.
It focuses your attention.
It informs the very firing and wiring
of your neurological makeup.
You make the commitment, then the commitment makes you.
Your commitment is the space in which you show up as action
to materially construct that which does not yet exist.
Notice, then, that power is not found in the current
circumstance; it is found in *you being committed*
to generate a new circumstance.
Your sincere commitment will leave you empowered
to generate whatever is necessary for the outcome you desire.

Experiment • Discover

Commitment is desire in motion.

NEW PERSPECTIVE AND POSSIBILITY

- Looking at my current actions alone, to what am I sincerely committed? To what am I not committed?

- In what ways do I resist commitment?

- What dreams of mine are in need of my genuine commitment?

- Based on what I desire to experience in life, what new commitment is needed in order to bring that about, and what action will I take as the demonstration of my new commitment?

Practice • Grow

WEEK 38

38

I choose to...

Speak on Purpose

Speaking is a creative act.
Always.
You get the experience you say you're having.
Always.
Your experience does not come directly from your situation;
it comes from what you *say* about your situation.
The experience you're having will be consistent
with what you're telling yourself about it.
You live in the world your words create.
With words, you build palaces just as easily as prisons.
Speak words that create the world you want to live in.
Be intentional with your words,
and you will be empowered
in every situation
to create the experience you're committed to having.

Experiment • Discover

With words, you build palaces just as easily as prisons.

NEW PERSPECTIVE AND POSSIBILITY

- What experiences do my words create for me?

- What experiences do my words create for others?

- How will I alter my words to reflect the world I desire to live in?

Practice • Grow

WEEK 39

39

I choose to...

Have Enough Time

In how you organize your life,
there are the things you choose to have time for
and the things you choose not to have time for.
You always have time for what's important to you.
If you don't have time for something,
it only means that it's not important to you right now.
That's it.
It's not right or wrong either way.
The perception that you don't have time for what you
want is an incredibly disempowered way to relate to life.
Truth is, you will always make time for what you really
want. "Not enough time" is a delusion.
You have all the time there is.
You spend that time on what's important to
you right now.

Experiment • Discover

You have all the time there is.

NEW PERSPECTIVE AND POSSIBILITY

- According to my current schedule, what's important to me right now?

- What things are actually important to me that I have neglected to allocate time for?

- To create having enough time for what I want, what must I stop? What must I start?

Practice • Grow

WEEK 40

I choose to...

Forgive

To forgive is to release, to set free.
I find that what prevents most people from forgiving someone
is the fear of being wronged
by that someone again.
Do not confuse forgiveness with trust.
Releasing someone for an offense
has nothing to do with trusting them again.
If you desire to remain in relationship with someone who has
broken trust with you, trust must be rebuilt.
Have they demonstrated, in action,
their commitment to *being trustworthy*?
Have they taken responsibility, in action,
for repairing the fracture?
Believe what a person's actions say about who they are.
Until their actions show you they are someone to be trusted, they
aren't. Where trust has not been rebuilt,
you are dealing with the same person who broke faith
with you to begin with. Until there is a sincere commitment,
demonstrated by action,
to restore and rebuild trust with you, the only thing you can
count on them for is more broken trust.
Forgiveness, however, is an entirely different matter than trust.
It has little to do with the other person and much to do with you.
To forgive is to stop ruminating, resenting, or retaliating over
an offense. To forgive is to cut loose the emotional and mental
ties binding you to the past and robbing you of your precious
energy and attention.
Love yourself too much
to ever withhold forgiveness from another.
Unforgiveness is a prison sentence you render
upon someone else for which you serve the time.
By condemning them, you imprison yourself.

By releasing them, you set yourself free.

Experiment • Discover

Unforgiveness is a prison sentence
you render upon someone else
for which you serve the time.

NEW PERSPECTIVE AND POSSIBILITY

- How do I distinguish trust from forgiveness?

- How does forgiveness feel in my body?

- How does unforgiveness feel in my body?

- What individual, community, or system will I forgive?

- What does it cost me to forgive?

- What does it cost me to *not* forgive?

- What is possible for me when I forgive?

Practice • Grow

WEEK 41

I choose to...

See
Opportunity

The way you relate to a situation
correlates with the way you see it.
And the way you see a situation
correlates with what you have decided about it.
In order to see opportunity,
you must first decide that opportunity exists.
Deciding that opportunity exists in a situation will have
you *seeing* the opportunity that exists in a situation.
This is how you intentionally train your brain
to see in a new way.
When you see opportunity,
you will move and act and create your life in a manner
consistent with that opportunity.

Experiment • Discover

Deciding that opportunity
exists will have you
seeing the opportunity that exists.

NEW PERSPECTIVE AND POSSIBILITY

- What opportunity will I decide to see starting now?

- What can I decide in my current circumstance to create the experience I desire next?

- What resources are already available and at my disposal?

- How must I see this situation so that it is consistent with my desired outcome?

Practice • Grow

WEEK 42

I choose to...

Ask for Help

Asking for help with your dream is inspiring.
It means you're up to something
beyond what you can do on your own.
Rather than a sign of weakness,
asking for help is a sign of commitment
to a life that's bigger than you. Rather than a burden,
your request is an opportunity for others to rise up
and live bigger than themselves as well.
A life of "look what I can do" can't even compare with
what's possible in the life of "look what we can do."
The great impact you are truly capable of making
will be fulfilled only with the help and support of others.
One of the most liberating and empowering requests
You will ever make is, "Would you help me?"

Experiment • Discover

> ## Asking for help is a sign of commitment
> ## to a life that's bigger than you.

NEW PERSPECTIVE AND POSSIBILITY

- What judgments about asking for help are slowing me down?

- What areas of my life will benefit from help?

- What benefits could result from asking for help with my dreams?

- In what ways is my request for help an opportunity for others?

Practice • Grow

WEEK 43

I choose to...

Learn
from
Failure

One of the first lessons taught in martial arts is
how to fall well—the tuck and roll.
This is to prevent injury and, more importantly, to
leverage the momentum of every fall for gaining an
advantage.
When done correctly, a person will land on their feet and
in a better position to advance against their opponent.
In life, there is a similar lesson to learn regarding failure
that will serve you tremendously.
Your problem isn't that you fail;
it's that you are not yet trained to fail well.
Stop trying *not* to fail; learn *how* to fail—learn to tuck and
roll. Instead of seeing failure as evidence that you'll never
get it right, see it as evidence of growth and progress.
Instead of interpreting failure as life screaming, "Give up!"
interpret it as life redirecting, saying, "Find another way."
Instead of experiencing failure
as life happening *against* you to prevent your success,
experience life as happening *for* you
to deliver the lessons and knowledge *you must have*
in order to succeed.
Failing well means recognizing failure as an advancement,
not an impediment, to your dreams and aspirations.
By leveraging everything failure brings your way,
you will gain an advantage in life
and position yourself to achieve what matters to you.

Experiment • Discover

Your problem isn't that you fail;
it's that you are not yet trained
to fail well.
Stop trying *not* to fail;
learn *how* to fail.

NEW PERSPECTIVE AND POSSIBILITY

- Is there room in my life for failure, or am I actively avoiding it?

- What has failure previously taught me?

- How will I use failure to advance my life?

- Who do I know who has failed spectacularly? What can I learn from them?

Practice • Grow

WEEK 44

I choose to...
Love
Extravagantly

The way you treat yourself is a template
for how you inevitably treat others.
There is a popular rumor that self-love is selfish. I have
great compassion for the person who started this rumor
and for all who have ever believed it.
Truth is, selfishness doesn't come from loving yourself;
selfishness comes from *not* loving yourself.
It is the *absence* of self-love that is selfish.
When you don't love yourself, you create a bottomless
pit of lack in your life, and no amount of love from
others will compensate for that deficit. Your default will
be selfishness with others, always taking more than you
give. When you withhold love from yourself, you can't
help but withhold love from others, as love will be limited
and scarce for you.
Conversely, when you love yourself, you create a perpetual
fountainhead of love in your life that will overflow
in you, through you, from you, and back to you,
multiplied.
Your default will be generosity—even sacrifice— with
others, freely giving more than you take.
When you extravagantly love yourself,
you can't help but extravagantly love others,
as love will abound in your life in every way.

Experiment • Discover

Selfishness doesn't come
from loving yourself;
selfishness comes from
not loving yourself.

NEW PERSPECTIVE AND POSSIBILITY

- How do I define love?

- In what ways do I withhold love?

- What if love is more than something I have? What if love is who I am?

- Is there any limit to love?

- What would I have to give up in order to love extravagantly?

Practice • Grow

WEEK 45

I choose to...

Release

Regarding great love, great loss, and great wrong,
it is common to struggle with letting go.
The struggle comes from a perception that
letting go is hard.
But that is a mistake about the source of difficulty.
Letting go isn't what's hard;
what's hard is persisting in holding on.
Letting go actually remedies the difficulty.
Regarding growth, one of the most important things you
must be vigilant to let go of is anything that has worked
for you in the past that no longer works now. There are
things that worked wonderfully to bring you to where
you are today that will not work for
where you want to go next.
In fact, continuing to hold on to something
that doesn't work for what's next
will only *interfere* with what's next.

Experiment • Discover

Letting go isn't what's hard;
what's hard is persisting in holding on.
Letting go actually remedies
the difficulty.

NEW PERSPECTIVE AND POSSIBILITY

- What concerns, resentments, and expectations would it serve me to release?

- How does my body feel when I let go?

- What good will I release into the world?

- What thinking, speaking, and actions have served me to this point that will not serve what I want next?

Practice • Grow

WEEK 46

I choose to...

Upgrade My Questions

The quality of your life is shaped by the questions you
ask. Questions operate as information filters
in the brain.
They set the conditions by which your brain sorts
through billions of available inputs to decide
which information is to be noticed and
which is to be ignored.
Much like programming a destination into a navigation
system, the question you ask sets your direction
and limits your outcome.
You'll wind up here and not there because the question
itself determines which options will and won't enter
your conscious awareness as being available to you.
Consider the difference in results produced
by the following two questions:
"Why is this happening to me?" vs.
"What will I create with this?"
A new question is a door to a new world of possibility.
You will powerfully transform the results you are getting
by employing questions you are not yet asking.
Upgrade your questions, and you'll upgrade your life.

Experiment • Discover

Powerfully transform the results
you are getting
by employing questions
you are not yet asking.

NEW PERSPECTIVE AND POSSIBILITY

- Which questions that I've often asked are no longer serving me?

- How might I upgrade the quality of questions I ask?

- What questions would help me create what's missing in my life?

- What question have I been afraid to ask myself?

- What question have I been afraid to ask others?

- What question would turn this situation around?

Practice • Grow

WEEK 47

47

I choose to...

Listen
Deeply

The source of what you hear is not your ears;
it's your mind.
When you listen deeply, without agenda and expectation,
your listening is a miraculous space that draws out the
deep, mysterious waters of the human heart.
In deep listening, new possibilities emerge and develop.
In deep listening, people become more fully who they are.
In deep listening, lives and situations transform.
But most of the time, it is rare for you to listen deeply
because you are usually listening *for* something instead.
There is a subtle, unconscious, preset agenda in your
listening. You listen for what is familiar
and what you already think you know.
You listen for what should and shouldn't be
in the conversation, for what you agree and disagree with,
or for who is right and who is wrong.
You listen for meaning according to your expectations
and previous experiences.
This unconscious agenda filters, colors,
and distorts what you hear, because you will always hear
what you're listening *for* to the exclusion
of what is actually being expressed.
Listening deeply removes that filter and opens your mind
to hear what you couldn't hear before.
Listening deeply is a powerful force,
as deep calls unto deep.
Listening deeply creates the instinctive experience for
others of being valued, appreciated, and loved
without saying a word.

Experiment • Discover

The source of what you hear is not your ears; it's your mind.

NEW PERSPECTIVE AND POSSIBILITY

- When I listen, what do I listen for?

- What keeps me from listening deeply to others?

- What do I hear when I listen without agenda or expectation?

- Who do I know who listens deeply?

- How do I feel when I am fully heard?

- What current situations am I facing that will be served by deep listening?

Practice • Grow

WEEK 48

48

I choose to...

Stop
Making
Excuses

When creating what matters to you in life,
there is a type of excuse you must be aware of. This
excuse is particularly sneaky because it hides
under a different name.
It's called a reason.
When it comes to not getting desired results,
reasons are just cleverly disguised excuses.
Reasons are *designer* excuses.
They are a socially acceptable way to feel better
about not getting the life you actually want.
Reasons for stopping. Reasons for quitting.
Reasons it didn't work out.
In life, you will either create what you want
or create a bunch of reasons why you didn't.
Just for a moment, imagine yourself doing everything
you say you will do, regardless of the reasons to do
otherwise.
When you stop making excuses,
you make yourself unstoppable.

Experiment • Discover

Reasons are *designer* excuses.
They are a socially acceptable way
to feel better
about not getting the life
you actually want.

NEW PERSPECTIVE AND POSSIBILITY

- What do I really want, and what will I likely do to keep from getting it?

- What reasons do I use for not having what I desire?

- What are my current excuses costing me?

- When I stop letting excuses stop me, what's possible?

Practice • Grow

WEEK 49

I choose to...

Complete
What
I Start

Trust in yourself is priceless.
Every decision you make rests on the foundation
of your trust in yourself.
When you trust yourself, your life advances.
When you do not trust yourself,
your life vacillates and falters.
Trust in yourself doesn't happen randomly;
it increases and decreases proportionately
to how you handle the things you start.
Quitting what you start will relieve you from any
unpleasantness in your current undertaking, be it
stress, anxiety, fatigue, frustration, discomfort, loneliness,
ridicule, fear, risk, or even boredom, AND it will silently
erode your capacity to accomplish the things you set
out to do.
Completing what you start will often get unpleasant,
especially as desired results are delayed
and enthusiasm wanes,
AND it will strengthen your capacity
to achieve anything you commit to in life.
This one principle alone
—complete whatever you start—
will have you moving mountains where others fail.

Experiment • Discover

Trust in yourself
doesn't happen randomly;
it increases and decreases
proportionately
to how you handle the things you start.

NEW PERSPECTIVE AND POSSIBILITY

- What have I left undone that, once completed, will be valuable for me or others?

- Where in my life do I quit rather than complete?

- What will it take, and how will I organize my life, in order to finish what I start?

Practice • Grow

WEEK 50

I choose to...

Receive

To get what you want in life you must be single-minded
in your openness to receive. That means congruence
between your conscious and subconscious brain.
One of the greatest sources of frustration you can ever
experience is the incongruence
of being open to receiving your desires consciously
while being closed to receiving them subconsciously.
So pay attention to the sensations
in your body
when you receive.
If you feel tension when receiving, whether it be receiving
a compliment, help, money, attention, or pleasure,
that is a strong indication
that you are subconsciously closed
to receiving in general.
It means you will subconsciously find ways to keep out
of your life the very things you consciously desire.
The key to receiving is congruence.
And the key to congruence is practice.
Practice receiving. Every day.
As you practice, notice the tension and contraction in your
body. Breathe through the tension and feel yourself relax
as you say thank you for whatever it is you are receiving.
Train your body to relax and enjoy as you receive.
Soon your body will feel energized when receiving.
This is an indicator of subconscious openness.
As receiving becomes familiar, comfortable, and even
enjoyable subconsciously, there will be a material difference
in how easily and quickly you attain your
conscious desires.

Experiment • Discover

One of the greatest sources
of frustration you can ever experience
is the incongruence
of being open
to receiving your desires consciously
while being closed
to receiving them subconsciously.

NEW PERSPECTIVE AND POSSIBILITY

- What do I find difficult to receive?

- What is it about receiving that feels awkward for me?

- How do others benefit when I'm willing to receive?

- How will I align my life to receive what I desire?

- What if receiving could be easy and fun?

- In what ways will I practice receiving today?

Practice • Grow

WEEK 51

I choose to...
Experience Miracles

A miracle for you is something that
appears impossible from your current perspective
that is *already* possible from another perspective.
Contrary to popular opinion, miracles aren't inherently
random or rare. You can actually make choices
that increase the miraculous in your life.
Really.
Organizing your life for miracles is not a license for
irresponsibility. This works to the degree you live with
integrity to keep and honor your word,
to be ruthlessly responsible in fulfilling your
commitments.
To experience miracles, you must take on situations,
opportunities, challenges, and commitments that look
impossible according to your current logic.
Miracles require you to make choices
that don't currently make sense.
Say yes to what you really want without the delay
of *figuring out* how you'll accomplish it first.
Step beyond the certainty of the knowledge and
understanding you already possess.
There usually are logical explanations for miracles,
but *that* level of logic lives beyond
your *current* level of logic.

Experiment • Discover

Miracles require you to make choices that don't currently make sense.

NEW PERSPECTIVE AND POSSIBILITY

- What is something I deeply desire and have been reluctant to pursue because I haven't yet figured out how to make it work?

- What "impossibility" will I say yes to today?

- In what ways does my current logic stop me?

- How am I positioning my life to experience miracles?

Practice • Grow

WEEK 52

I choose to...

Start
Again

For anything substantial, the hardest and slowest part
of growth is the beginning. I call it the
underground work.
It is everything that must first be established
before getting to ground level.
This is as true for buildings and businesses as it is for
relationships and plants. The deeper and wider the
foundation, the stronger, higher, bigger, as well as more
productive, enduring, and resilient the result.
Once an endeavor reaches ground level,
growth is comparatively fast and easy.
Notice this.
When disaster strikes and everything visible is
destroyed,
as long as the foundation remains,
starting again is *not* starting back at the beginning;
it is starting at ground level, which is the fast
and easy part.
Starting at ground level is exponentially more advanced
than starting at the beginning.
Consider your underground work—your roots, your
foundation. What have you learned?
What remains with you?
You are further along
than your present conditions may suggest.

Experiment • Discover

Starting again is not starting
back at the beginning;
it is starting at ground level,
which is the fast and easy part.

NEW PERSPECTIVE AND POSSIBILITY

- What limits and judgments have I made against starting again?

- If success were guaranteed, would I start again, no matter how many times I fail along the way?

- What benefits do I see for myself in starting again?

Practice • Grow

Acknowledgements

To the Creator of all—You are life, and you are love. I create because You Are.

Padre and Mumsy—thank you for faithfully guiding and loving your strong-willed child. I do not envy that responsibility.

Charlie—your love and big brain inspire new possibility in my life every day. Your encouragement and support turn my ideas into reality. Sweet man, who you are just lights me up.

Carissa DeAngelis, Joe Keffer, Talena Martinez, and Becky Trussell Williams—your ruthless feedback on the rough, rough, rough initial manuscript made *Intentional* more accessible and more readable to more people than it ever would have reached without you.

Jara Kern and Elite Authors—thank you for transforming *Intentional* into a coherent expression that others can understand and enjoy.

Olivier Darbonville—you made *Intentional* a delight for the eyes as well as the mind.

Ephraim Olschewski—you introduced me to a world of creating I didn't know that I didn't know existed and coached me in how to powerfully live there. That changed everything for me.

And each of my clients—our conversations together have been the fuel and fodder for every page of this book. I probably owe you some royalties. It's an honor to witness the commitment, courage, and grit you bring to intentionally creating your life every day.

Coming Work

There is a possibility in life that I would like to introduce to you. This possibility is the music I have been called to bring forth and orchestrate as my service in the world. And it is the source from which *Intentional* was inspired and written for you. *Intentional* is an essential piece of this larger composition as well as a fundamental practice for accessing it as a way of life.

Over the past twenty years, I have worked with thousands of people and have observed that most human beings share a desire for a particular kind of life, a particular quality of life. Interestingly, this desire remains unarticulated, unnamed, and unexperienced by the majority of us who hunger for it. It's a life of "just right" when it comes to the things that are important to us.

You may even be looking for it right now.

Remember *Goldilocks*? The porridge: Too hot! Too cold! Ahh, just right! The bed: Too hard! Too soft! Ahh, just right!

Consistently, when it comes to the things we desire, human nature is just like that of Goldilocks. We are looking for "just right" in love, significance, wealth, health, productivity, power, possessions, time, experiences, etc.

Frustratingly, the lived experience for most of us is to vacillate between some version of never enough, barely enough, and too much.

Rarely do we ever experience "just right," right?

So it would be normal to think of "just right" as a hard-to-find balance between extreme negatives. But I say that "just right" is not a midway point between opposites on the spectra of scarcity and excess, poverty and exorbitance, or deprivation and overindulgence. When it comes to what's important to you, "just right" transcends these spectra altogether. "Just right" is a unique dimension of life unto itself, tailored to each person and quantified by who they are committed to being in the world.

I call this "just right" dimension of life Plenteousness.
Plenteousness is the abiding state of More Than Enough:
Nothing Missing and
Never Too Much.

A life of Plenteousness—The Plenteous Life—is one of creating and experiencing more than enough of what's important and desirable without it being so much that it brings trouble, hassle, or destruction along with it. There is always extra, and generosity is a joy. Plenteousness will be shaped by one's purpose and commitments; therefore, that which constitutes Plenteousness for you will inherently be different from what constitutes Plenteousness for me.

Imagine eliminating scarcity, strain, and stagnation in your life. Imagine the experience of actually getting ahead, advancing, and making progress.

Imagine living in the fullness of More Than Enough:
Nothing Missing and
Never Too Much
in every way that matters to *you*.

Plenteousness is not a fairy tale; it is an actual reality that is accessible and achievable for you. The Plenteous Life is fully within your capacity to produce...once you consciously choose that it be so.

Conscious choosing is *the* primary step for generating The Plenteous Life. And *Intentional* is a powerful tool to help you master conscious choosing as a skill for creating more of what matters to you for the rest of your life.

More tools—books, courses, programs—for The Plenteous Life are being developed right now! Join TPL Community here:

www.plenteouslife.com

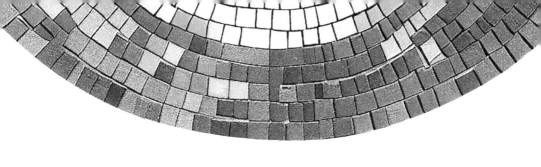

We need more people who are thrilled to be alive.

— **Becky Henderson**

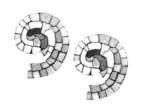

About
THE AUTHOR

"I help The Innovator Leader create more than enough of what matters to them."

Becky Henderson is creator, founder, and principal coach of The Plenteous Life, a system of advanced personal mastery tools and services for professionals committed to growth, vitality, and purpose.

Since 1996, Becky has been an executive coach, professional counselor, and mentor in the field of human transformation and development. From former sex slaves to CEOs, students to professionals, not-for-profit to corporate companies, Becky has assisted in the transformation of over 20,000 people both domestically and internationally. She is extraordinary at empowering others to own and operate in their God-given capacity to create what matters to them.

Becky holds an MA in counseling psychology from The University of Texas at Tyler and is a Licensed Professional Counselor (LPC) in the state of Texas. As an Executive Transformation Coach, Becky helps The Innovator Leader eliminate the three greatest threats to their impact and productivity—scarcity, strain, and stagnation—leaving them unstoppable in doing what they were born to do.

Becky lives in Austin, Texas. She loves live music, salsa dancing, traveling the globe, and laughing with—and at—her smartass husband.

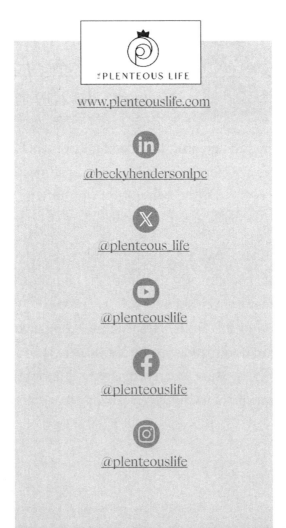

www.plenteouslife.com

@beckyhendersonlpc

@plenteous_life

@plenteouslife

@plenteouslife

@plenteouslife

Printed in Great Britain
by Amazon

33565657R00145